GOOD ★ SPORTS
BY GLENN STOUT

ABLE TO PLAY

GOOD★SPORTS

BY GLENN STOUT

ABLE TO PLAY

OVERCOMING PHYSICAL CHALLENGES

sandpiper

HOUGHTON MIFFLIN HARCOURT
BOSTON NEW YORK 2012

Library of Congress Cataloging-in-Publication Data
Stout, Glenn, 1958–
Able to play : overcoming physical challenges / by Glenn Stout.
    p. cm. — (Good sports)
ISBN 978-0-547-41733-2
1. Baseball players with disabilities—United States—Biography—Juvenile
literature.   I. Title.
GV865.A1S815 2012
796.3570922—dc23
[B]
2011020502

Manufactured the United States of America
DOC 10 9 8 7 6 5 4 3 2

4500359939

★

*This book is dedicated to everyone who
tries hard and gives his or her best effort.*

CONTENTS

INTRODUCTION

No one is perfect. And though each of us has flaws and problems, we are defined by how we live our lives. Our limitations are not who we are.

Those who have a physical condition that affects his or her ability to do something were once referred to as either "crippled," "handicapped," or "disabled," all words that focused on what a person could not do rather than what they could. Some people with a physical disability, disease, or impairment were often shunted aside and not even allowed the opportunity to prove what they could accomplish.

Fortunately, today we realize that everyone is different.

With practice, hard work, and determination, each of us can turn a disability into a challenge that can be overcome.

I know this myself. I write for a living, but I have a nerve problem with one of my hands that makes it hard for me to make my fingers go precisely where I tell them to go. As a result, I cannot type using all my fingers like most other writers. I once took a test that said because of this problem, I should not try to be a writer. I ignored the test and followed my dream. I have learned to type using just a few fingers and have since written and published millions of words.

Although it might not always be possible to do *everything* you want to do, the ballplayers profiled in *Able to Play* demonstrate that it is always worth trying. If you don't try, you will never know just how much you can achieve.

Pitcher Mordecai "Three Finger" Brown became one of the greatest pitchers in baseball despite losing most of a finger in a farming accident.

MORDECAI BROWN AND THE CURVEBALL

THERE IS AN OLD SAYING THAT GOES, "Sometimes life throws you a curveball," which means life might not always be easy or go according to plan. That is exactly what happened to young Mordecai (MORE-duh-kye) Brown. Yet just because life threw Mordecai a curveball, he didn't give up. In fact, he learned to use his misfortune to help *throw* a curveball.

Born Mordecai Peter Centennial Brown in 1876 and named after the nation's centennial, Mordecai was raised on a farm in rural Indiana. One day when he was five years old, his life changed.

It began just like any other day. Mordecai and his older

brother were doing their daily chores, helping out on the farm.

The boys' uncle kept livestock, and Mordecai and his brother liked to help with the feeding and care of the animals. On this particular day they had to prepare the feed. Instead of just giving the livestock bales of hay or cornstalks, Mordecai and his brother first had to chop the feed up so it would be easier for the animals to digest. They used a machine called a feed cutter.

The feed cutter used a series of sharp, circular blades that chopped the feed into small pieces. Mordecai's brother, being older and stronger, turned the crank on the machine that spun a series of gears and pulleys that made the blades spin and go up and down quickly. Mordecai's job was to place the feed in a chute that delivered it to the blades.

The boys had used the machine many times before and never had any trouble. On this day, however, something went wrong.

Mordecai might have become distracted or placed too much feed into the chute, but as he reached down and pushed the feed ahead, he went too far. The razor-sharp blades closed down on the fingers of his right hand.

Suddenly, all Mordecai and his brother saw was blood.

Mordecai instantly screamed out in pain and his brother immediately stopped cranking the machine. He helped Mordecai free his hand, but it was too late. Mordecai was badly cut, and blood spewed out everywhere. As Mordecai later recalled, his fingers were "chopped to ribbons."

The screams of Mordecai and his brother brought his uncle running to their aid. Deep gashes ran across Mordecai's right hand. His index, or pointing, finger hung limply by the skin.

His uncle quickly wrapped Mordecai's hand with cloth to slow the bleeding, bundled him up, put him in the back of a farm wagon, then harnessed one of his horses to the wagon and took off for the nearby town of Nyesville. Mordecai managed to stifle his tears and stayed nearly silent as the horse and wagon bounced over the dirt road toward town.

The town physician, Doc Gillum, had served as a surgeon in the Civil War. He was accustomed to treating severe injuries and it took him only a moment to assess the damage. Doc Gillum realized it would be impossible to save Mordecai's finger.

He gave the young boy some medicine to ease his pain

and help him stay calm while Gillum cleaned the wounds. Then the doctor took out a sharp instrument and cut the damaged finger loose below the first knuckle, leaving only a short stump behind, and carefully sewed a flap of skin over the end. Several other fingers were broken and cut, so the doctor sewed together the wounds then applied splints to each finger to hold them straight while they healed. Then he wrapped the hand with bandages. Mordecai would live, but he would go through life with only three full fingers on his right hand.

Five weeks later Mordecai's fingers were still in splints and his hand was still wrapped in bandages, but he was healing quickly. At times he completely forgot that he had been in an accident. He was more interested in playing than worrying about his hand.

One day Mordecai and his sister wondered if rabbits could swim. To find out, they filled a tub with water and dropped their pet rabbit into the water. Although rabbits can swim, they don't like being in the water and the bunny began thrashing around. Little Mordecai leaned over into the tub toward the rabbit then tumbled in headfirst. As he did he instinctively reached out with his injured hand.

He broke his fall but felt sharp pains in his injured hand. When he unwrapped the bandages he saw that his fingers, particularly his middle finger, were bent and swollen. He had hurt his hand again, breaking six bones in his fingers.

"Don't tell Dad!" he told his sister. Mordecai was afraid that if his father found out he had broken his fingers that he would get in trouble. So instead of going to the doctor and having the fingers straightened out and placed in a splint, Mordecai gritted his teeth and bandaged the hand himself.

A few weeks later, when the bandages finally came off for good, he realized that was a mistake. Although the stump of the amputated finger and his cuts had healed, he could no longer straighten his little finger and his other fingers were bent and misshapen. His middle finger, in particular, zigzagged like a lightning bolt, bending first to the left and then to the right. When Doc Gillum got a look at it he thought about breaking the finger again to set it straight, but he decided Mordecai had been through enough. He would leave the finger as it was—and leave Mordecai with a permanently damaged hand.

It would turn out to be the best thing that ever happened. Mordecai Peter Centennial Brown would soon find fame—and a new nickname.

★ ★ ★

Mordecai adapted quickly to the loss of his finger. Despite the disfigurement he learned to do almost everything everyone else did, including holding a pencil to write. The Browns treated Mordecai the same as they treated their other children, and he continued to do his chores on the farm. If he found a task difficult to do with his damaged hand, he either used his left hand or figured out a new way to do it with his right, using his middle finger for things he had previously done with his index finger.

Like most young boys, Mordecai didn't work all the time. One of his favorite things to do was throw rocks and anything else he could get his hands on at the farm, like potatoes. After his chores were done he would spend hours throwing rocks and other objects at the barn, trying to knock out the knots in the wood. He was just having fun. He didn't realize that he was developing a skill that would change his life.

Most people throw rocks or other objects, like a ball, by placing their thumb underneath it and their index and middle fingers on top. When they release it, the object spins backwards off the fingers. Mordecai, of course, didn't have an index finger, but by putting his bent middle finger and his ring finger on top of the ball, he could still throw. Mordecai didn't mind that the ball spun sideways a little bit, sometimes dipping a little at the end. He soon became accustomed to throwing that way and over time learned to hit his target, whether he was throwing a stone, a potato, or a ball.

Growing up in the country provided few opportunities for Mordecai to learn a trade or start a career, and his family could not afford to send him to college. Most young men around Nyesville worked on the family farm or in one of the nearby coal mines.

When Mordecai was fourteen, he stopped going to school and got a job working at the John Batty coal mine in Nyesville. Although most mine employees worked underground digging coal and helping to bring it to the surface, Mordecai was more fortunate. He was smart and good with numbers and was able to avoid the dangerous work deep in the mine. He was hired instead to work on the surface as what is known as a checker, keeping daily records of the mine, such as how much coal was dug each day and which workers were on the job.

Still, the days were often long and difficult. Mordecai and many other miners looked forward to quitting time, when they got together to play or watch baseball.

Baseball was important in the community. There were no movie theaters or many other things to do for entertainment, so after work and on the weekends nearly the whole town went to the ballpark. Games that pitted teams from different mines or different towns often attracted big crowds. The mine owners, miners, and local residents often bet on the outcome and passed a hat through the crowd to pay the players. When the weather was good, a young man could play baseball almost every day of the week, and pick up a few extra dollars at the same time.

Mordecai was a talented young player and soon found his place on several different local teams. A good hitter, Mordecai had little trouble holding the bat with his damaged hand. In fact, he was a switch hitter, batting left-handed against right-handed pitchers and right-handed against lefties. He was a good fielder, too, and primarily played third base. His throwing arm, despite the injuries to his hand, was strong. The only difficulty he had throwing was the unusual spin his damaged fingers put on the ball, which gave the ball a natural break or sinking action. However, throwing all those stones at the barn had taught Mordecai how to control his throws.

After a few years Mordecai was one of the best players in Nyesville and one of the best players on the mine team. Sometimes his boss at the mine would even hire another man to do Mordecai's job to give him more time to play ball. He was soon recruited to play for the Coxville Reds in the nearby mining town of Coxville.

Although Mordecai wasn't a professional ballplayer who earned his living entirely from baseball, he had become what is known as a semi-professional, a ballplayer who was given a job and paid a small sum of money to play baseball after work. Games between semipro teams often drew hundreds of fans.

In 1898, when Mordecai was twenty-two years old, the Coxville Reds traveled to play their arch rivals in Brazil, Indiana, a far more experienced team. More than bragging rights were at stake. Backers of each team put up one hundred dollars on the game. The winning team would split sixty dollars, while the losers would divide up only forty dollars.

Mordecai and his teammates weren't paid as well as the team from Brazil. They badly needed the money.

By game time hundreds of fans from both towns lined the field. What happened next isn't precisely clear, but the usual Coxville pitcher, a man named Clayton, was either too ill to play or left the game ill after only two innings.

Reds manager Jonny Buckley didn't want to cancel the game, disappoint the fans, or lose an opportunity to earn some extra money. He looked over at his team, and his eyes focused on Mordecai Brown.

Buckley knew that Mordecai had a strong and accurate arm. Although Mordecai had never really pitched before, Buckley walked up to him and said, "Brownie, we're up against it. You'll have to pitch the game."

Brown just looked at him and started sputtering, trying to think of reasons why he couldn't pitch, but Buckley wouldn't listen. "You have the best arm on the team," he explained.

That was the day Mordecai's life changed. He didn't want to disappoint his team so he reluctantly took the ball and headed to the pitching rubber. He wound up carefully and threw a few practice pitches, telling himself just to throw strikes. "All I had was smoke," he told a sportswriter later, meaning all he knew how to do was rear back and throw a fastball.

The Brazil batters could hardly wait to face him. They were delighted to face an inexperienced pitcher.

Batter after batter walked confidently up to the plate, but they soon found themselves headed back to the dugout. Mordecai's fastball wasn't even that fast, but he had good control. More importantly, however, was that every pitch he threw sank just as it crossed the plate, making it difficult for the Brazil hitters to meet the ball squarely. Batter after batter beat the ball into the ground for easy ground ball outs.

The stump of his amputated finger affected Mordecai's grip on the ball, and just as every throw he made from third base swerved and dipped, so did each of his pitches.

Mordecai Brown pitched seven full innings and not a single Brazil hitter reached first base. Coxville won, 9-3, and after the game the Coxville fans surrounded Brown, pounding him on the back and offering their congratulations. "I was the idol of Coxville," he later recalled. "That just naturally made me lose my head and right then and there I began to be a pitcher in my own mind." Although he dreamed about playing professional baseball, and even playing in the National League, the only major league in existence at the time, Mordecai know the odds were against him. After all, who would take a chance on a pitcher with only three fingers?

After he pitched a few more games the manager of the Brazil team approached Mordecai and offered him more money than he was making pitching for Coxville. Mordecai pitched the next season for Brazil and soon every baseball fan in western Indiana was talking about the great pitcher Mordecai Brown.

For the next two seasons Mordecai won game after game, easily beating other town and mine teams, earning as much as ten dollars a game. By pitching several times a week he earned enough to quit his job and play full-time.

The more he pitched the better he became. Over time Mordecai learned that by changing the angle of his arm he could change the way the ball moved. When he threw overhand, the ball tended to move sideways, but when he dropped his arm lower and threw from three quarters or sidearm, his pitches sank. When he threw underhand, the ball seemed to rise on its way to the plate. He also learned to keep the batter off balance by changing speeds, throwing one pitch fast and the next pitch slow.

In 1901 a new minor league was created, officially known as the Illinois-Indiana-Iowa League because each team was based in one of those three states. Usually referred to as the Three-I League, they placed a team nicknamed the Hottentots in nearby Terre Haute, Indiana, and the club held a tryout. They were particularly interested in pitchers.

Mordecai's friends urged him to try out and he agreed. He knew this could be his big chance. When he arrived at the Terre Haute ballpark he discovered he was one of twelve men trying out for three pitching spots.

For the next hour or so Mordecai and the other hurlers took turns throwing for Hottentot manager Bill Krieg. Mordecai felt that he threw well, but the manager was unimpressed. Although the Three-I League was just a minor league, it was still professional baseball and Krieg probably didn't believe Brown threw fast enough. He might also have thought Mordecai's damaged hand would prevent him from succeeding. Getting hitters out in semipro baseball was one thing, but getting out a professional hitter was more difficult. Besides, Mordecai was twenty-four, old for a rookie. Krieg cut Mordecai from the team.

Mordecai was disappointed. When he returned home and told his friends from the mines, they got angry. They all believed in him.

Six hundred fans signed a petition asking the Terre Haute manager to reconsider and put Mordecai on the team. If he didn't, those six hundred baseball fans promised to boycott the Hottentots. The new team could not afford to lose that many fans so Krieg changed his mind. He signed Mordecai to a contract for sixty dollars a month.

Mordecai Brown was now a professional baseball player, but he still was a long way from making the major leagues.

The Three-I League was known as a D league, the lowest minor league classification in the country. Most of the players were either inexperienced young boys just off the farm or older players of limited ability on their way down. Few had any real chance of having a long career in professional baseball. Even though there was now a second major league, the American League, reaching the majors remained a distant dream.

Still, becoming a professional player meant everything to Mordecai Brown. He knew if he succeeded in baseball he might never have to work at the mine again.

When the regular season started, Mordecai soon realized that the level of play in the Three-I League was much better than what he was accustomed to. Although few other pitchers could match his control, some threw harder and almost all of them threw a curveball. As he later told a newspaper reporter, "I worked hard and watched other pitchers, studying their styles, and trying to learn how to pitch." He was a fast learner and was soon one of the better pitchers in the league.

Mordecai soon realized that his sinking fastball and good control would not be enough for him to succeed as a professional. He would have to learn how to throw a curveball.

A thrown baseball curves or drops due to a combination of gravity and the way air interacts with the stitches on the spinning ball. As the seams of the baseball strike the air, they change the air pressure around the ball. Combined with the natural fall the ball takes due to gravity and the angle of the pitcher's motion, the ball can both drop and curve at the same time. To the hitter, a good curveball appears to swerve and drop a foot or more at the last moment, making it very difficult to hit. The more spin a pitcher can put on the ball, the more the pitch will break.

Although young players should not try to throw curveballs, Mordecai's arm was strong. He had never thrown the pitch before, but once he saw how much success other pitchers had throwing curveballs, he was determined to learn.

There was just one problem. Most pitchers throw a curveball by turning their hand to the side, so that instead of the ball rolling off the fingertips of their first two fingers, they bring their first two fingers over the top of the baseball and the ball rolls off the side of the first finger and rotates toward the hitter. Mordecai, however, didn't have a first finger.

That didn't stop him. Just as he had learned how to throw accurately with his damaged hand by throwing rocks at the barn, Mordecai began trying to throw a curveball, practicing the pitch over and over again, trying different ways of holding the ball.

Since he didn't have a first finger, he had to use his middle finger to put spin on the ball. It was awkward at first, but he soon figured out that if he held the ball between his middle finger and thumb and wedged it against the stump of his first finger, he could grip the ball tightly enough to put spin on it using only his middle finger. Even better, with practice he realized that the way his middle finger was bent actually made it easier for him to throw a curveball. Mordecai's pitch curved dramatically, much more than that of most other pitchers.

Still, Mordecai waited to use the pitch. As he described later, he brought out his curveball for the first time "in the middle of a game." One particular hitter had been giving him trouble, and Mordecai had been trying to get him out by slinging the ball underhand. Then, as he said later, "I decided to take a chance." Instead of throwing underhand, Mordecai wound up and threw an overhand curveball, snapping his wrist as he released the pitch, bringing his middle finger over the top of the ball and spinning it off the side.

As the ball approached the hitter it seemed to be floating right over the middle of the plate. The batter's eyes grew wide and he started to take a big swing.

"Oof!" The batter took a hard swing over the top of the baseball as the ball dropped and curved away. "Strike!" called the umpire.

Mixing a few curveballs in with his fastballs made Mordecai much more difficult to hit. Even when batters did make contact, they often hit the ball weakly. The pitch was a success—and so was Mordecai.

Later that season, while Mordecai pitched a game in Rockford, Illinois, a scout for Omaha of the Western League, one of the best minor leagues in baseball, was watching a game between Rockford and Terre Haute. He had come to see another player, but he was more impressed with Mordecai. Terre Haute won the league championship and Mordecai finished the year with a record of 24–8, one of the best records in the league. After the season Mordecai signed a contract to play for Omaha in 1902.

It was a big change but armed with his new curveball Mordecai kept getting better. Even more experienced hitters found it difficult to get a hit against Mordecai. He finished every game he started for Omaha, once pitching three consecutive doubleheaders, and won twenty-seven games while losing only fifteen!

His performance got everyone's attention, and soon sportswriters all around the league were writing about the new pitching sensation they called "Three Finger" Brown. At the end of the season the St. Louis Cardinals of the National League signed Brown to a contract worth four hundred dollars a month. At the age of twenty-six, Three Finger Brown was a big leaguer.

But he did more than just make the major leagues. Brown lasted twelve seasons in the major leagues for the Cardinals, Chicago Cubs, and Cincinnati Reds, once leading the league with twenty-seven wins. He helped the Cubs to four pennants and two world championships and to win five games in the World Series, including three by shutout.

Another person might have never even tried to throw a baseball after losing a finger, but as Mordecai "Three Finger" Brown put it, "That old paw served me pretty well in its time." In 1949 Mordecai was elected to the National Baseball Hall of Fame.

Third baseman Ron Santo of the Cubs was one of the best players in baseball in the 1960s. He played virtually his entire career while suffering from diabetes.

RON SANTO'S BIG SECRET

RON SANTO WAS ON TOP of the world.

In the summer of 1958 the eighteen-year-old native of Seattle, Washington, had recently graduated from Franklin High School where he had been one of the greatest high school athletes in Washington state history. Santo earned six varsity letters as a member of the Franklin Quakers football and basketball teams, but baseball was his best sport. A catcher, he was named to the All City team three times and led his team to three straight league championships. His high school career culminated when he was named to the Hearst High School All-Star team and traveled to New York City to play in a high school all-star game at the Polo Grounds, then the home of the New York Giants of the National League.

By the time he returned to Seattle nearly every major league team was eager to sign Ron Santo to a contract. Today, a player of Santo's ability would be subjected to the baseball draft and only one team would have the right to sign him, but there was no draft in 1958. Teams bid against one another trying to convince Ron to sign with them.

The Cleveland Indians offered him a fifty-thousand-dollar bonus, and the Cincinnati Reds offered him eighty thousand dollars. He was flattered, but Ron didn't want to play for the Indians or the Reds.

As Santo later wrote, "I had become pretty friendly with the Cubs scout, Dave Kosher, and I was confident he was going to come through." Ron was a big baseball fan and despite the fact that the Chicago Cubs had not won the World Series since 1908, they were Ron's favorite team. He knew their history and dreamed about playing in their ballpark, beautiful Wrigley Field, where the outfield walls are covered with ivy. He also knew that the club needed help and figured his best chance to reach the big leagues fast would be with Chicago.

Kosher had learned how much money the other teams were offering and told Ron that the Cubs couldn't afford to offer a large bonus. He could only offer Ron twenty thousand dollars.

Ron didn't care. As he later explained in his biography, "My mind was made up. I was signing with the Cubs. To me, $20,000 was the same as $50,000 or $80,000. It was all a lot of money." He signed the contract and could not have been happier. By then, however, it was too late in the year for him to play. The Cubs told him to report to spring training in February of 1959.

Just before Ron reported to camp his mother sent him to his family physician, Dr. Tupper, for a checkup. Dr. Tupper took a routine blood test and soon returned to the office to give Ron the results.

Tupper liked Ron and usually greeted him with a big smile. This time, however, the doctor looked grim. Ron's blood test revealed an abnormality. "Ron," he said, "we found some sugar in your blood. You may have diabetes." According to the test, Ron had a form of diabetes known as type 1.

When a person who doesn't have diabetes eats something, the sugar in the food, known as glucose, stimulates the pancreas, an organ in the body, to release insulin into the blood. Insulin helps move the sugar and other nutrients into the cells of the body, where they are converted into energy. But people with type 1 diabetes don't produce enough insulin to move all the sugar into the cells and the sugar builds up in the blood. As a result the cells of the body run short of energy. Unless a person with diabetes is provided with extra insulin they can be plagued by fatigue and even pass out. Over time the disease can cause many other health complications.

Ron didn't know any of this. In fact, he didn't even know what diabetes was. He asked the doctor the only question on his mind: "Can I still play baseball?" Ron's doctor looked him straight in the eye. "I don't know," he said.

After leaving the doctor's office Ron went right to the public library and read everything he could about the disease. He learned that although diabetes could be managed through a strict diet and insulin shots to make sure his blood sugar levels remained constant, he would have to pay close attention to his body. Today, diabetic patients can easily monitor their blood sugar levels with a simple blood test they can give themselves, but when Ron was diagnosed no such tests were available. Living with diabetes was much more difficult than it is today. Ron learned that if he was not careful, the disease could cause him to go blind or lead to kidney failure or other serious health problems. Then Ron read something that really frightened him.

At the time the life expectancy for someone after they were diagnosed with diabetes was only twenty-five years.

Ron could hardly believe it. He felt perfectly healthy and didn't have any obvious visible symptoms of the disease, like intense fatigue or thirst. He couldn't understand how he could be so sick when he felt fine. In twenty-five years he hoped to be at the end of a long and successful baseball career; he didn't expect to be confronting his own death.

At the time, Ron knew of no other professional athletes who had diabetes. There was no one to answer the question "Can I still play baseball?" He would have to discover that answer himself.

Ron was determined to try. Afraid he would be cut from the team if the Cubs found out he had diabetes, Ron and his family kept the diagnosis a secret. But before he left Seattle for spring training, Ron attended a two-week clinic at a Seattle hospital to learn how to live with the disease.

Ron thought if he could avoid taking insulin he could keep his secret. At first, he was encouraged by what he learned. Doctors told him that by controlling his food intake, watching his diet, and exercising, he could help keep his blood sugar levels low.

One incident at the clinic, however, showed just how difficult living with the disease could be. He was attending a small class when another patient, a woman sitting next to him, suddenly passed out and slumped to the floor. Her blood sugar level had dropped and she had fainted.

Ron was still learning about diabetes and assumed it was because the woman was not yet on insulin. Then he learned that she was on insulin, yet had lost consciousness anyway.

Concerned, Ron asked a doctor, "Are you telling me I could be playing third base at Wrigley Field and just pass out?"

The doctor nodded, then explained, "You'll have symptoms first, and you have to learn what they are." He went on to tell Ron that when his blood sugar dropped to a dangerous level, he might begin to feel nauseated or light-headed. His skin might start to look pale and he might even have trouble seeing. If any of those things happened to Ron, he would have to eat something sweet, like a candy bar, to raise his blood sugar. If he did not, he could pass out and slip into a diabetic coma. If untreated, he could die. And no matter how careful Ron tried to be, over time the disease would only get worse. Even though Ron did not yet need to take insulin, the doctor told him it was inevitable.

While he was still concerned, Ron believed that as long as he was careful, he could still play baseball. He reported to spring training in February of 1959 absolutely thrilled to be a professional baseball player. He told no one that he had diabetes.

At first, training camp was a little confusing. Ron was one of dozens of young Cub prospects attending spring training, and for the first time in his life, baseball was a full-time job. Ron not only had to adjust to the long hours, but he had to learn to play a new position. The Cubs had too many catchers and asked Ron to play third base.

One day at camp Cubs coach Rogers Hornsby, one of the greatest hitters of all time and a member of the National Baseball Hall of Fame, gathered the young prospects together and bluntly told them what he thought of their hitting abilities. Hornsby, whose career batting average of .358 is the second highest in the history of baseball, knew what he was talking about.

Hornsby was blunt, and told almost every young player that he didn't think they had a chance to hit in the major leagues. Then he stopped in front of Ron.

"And you, kid," he said, "can hit in the big leagues." Ron was thrilled.

Ron was sent to the Cubs double-A farm team in San Antonio, Texas, for the 1959 season. After a slow start he began to hit the way Hornsby expected. Despite the fact that he was one of the youngest players on the team at age nineteen, and adjusting to a new position, he led the team in hitting with a .327 batting average to go along with eleven home runs and eighty-seven RBIs.

More important, however, Ron stayed healthy and was able to keep his diabetes a secret. In 1960 Ron was assigned to the Cubs' triple-A team in Houston. He played well and in June was called up to the major leagues by the Cubs.

When he joined, the team manager Lou Boudreau looked him in the eye and said, "There are ninety-five games left in the season. You'll be in all of them." The Cubs had decided that Ron would get every chance to succeed, and Ron knew he had to do well. He hoped that if he played well, the Cubs would be understanding if they found out he had diabetes.

He made his debut for the Cubs in a doubleheader in Pittsburgh. He got off to a great start, cracking out three hits, knocking in five runs, and leading the Cubs to two wins.

In 1961, after a decent rookie season in which he hit .251 with nine home runs, Ron demonstrated that he might one day become a star, cracking twenty-three home runs and hitting .284. Ron had gotten married, and after the season he and his wife moved to Chicago. Ron planned on being a Cub for a long time.

Up to that point, as Ron later recalled, he had succeeded in "fooling" the Cub doctors. He had been very careful, and no one suspected he had diabetes.

But that winter, Ron started experiencing pain in one of his legs. Then he started losing weight and had to go to the bathroom all the time. He knew that his diabetes was beginning to give him trouble.

By the time Ron went to a doctor he had lost more than twenty pounds. Ron explained that he was the Cubs third baseman and made the doctor promise to keep his illness a secret. "I've made the big leagues with diabetes," he explained. "I don't want people to know. I'm scared." Ron still wasn't sure how the Cubs would react.

The doctor immediately gave Ron an injection of insulin and taught Ron how to give himself his own injections twice each day, and how to tell if his blood sugar had dropped. In Ron's case, he learned that one of the first symptoms was a cold sweat. Then his tongue and nose would begin to feel numb, and as his body ran out of energy he would begin to feel light-headed and dizzy. If that happened, Ron had to eat or drink sugar immediately. The doctor told Ron that he always had to have a candy bar or some orange juice available.

Ron realized he had to take his disease seriously. Even though he wanted to keep the disease a secret, he also knew that he had to tell someone so if he passed out, they would know why. When he reported to the Cubs that spring he sensed that he could trust the team physician, Dr. Jacob Suker, and Ron told Suker that he had diabetes. The doctor understood Ron's concerns and promised to keep his secret.

But Suker didn't travel with the team on road trips, so just before the start of the regular season he told his roommate, catcher Cuno Barragan. Ron explained that he had to carry insulin and syringes with him so he could take his daily shot, and told Cuno about his symptoms.

The young catcher understood. "You can count on me." Barragan kept a close watch on Ron over the course of the year, and if he thought Ron was looking a little pale, he would remind him to have a piece of candy. Ron, however, had a difficult time adjusting to taking insulin and keeping such a close watch on his body. Although he still cracked seventeen home runs, his batting average tumbled to only .227.

Still, for the first time in many years it appeared as if the

Cubs had the makings of a winning team. Ron was one of a number of good young players on the team, such as outfielders Billy Williams and Lou Brock, both of whom would eventually be named to the National Baseball Hall of Fame, as would shortstop Ernie Banks. Cubs second baseman Ken Hubbs was the National League Rookie of the Year. The future was beginning to look bright—if Ron could remain healthy.

In 1963 Ron adjusted to taking insulin and responded with a performance that earned him a spot on the 1963 All-Star team and was also named the Cubs' team captain. After several long years of struggle, he finally felt that he had established himself as a major league baseball player. For the first time in his career he felt secure enough to tell the Cubs about his medical condition.

Ron met with Cubs general manager John Holland and told him everything he could about his disease. Holland understood, and the two men decided it would be a good idea for Ron to tell the entire team.

The general manager called a meeting in the Cubs clubhouse before a game. As Ron's teammates sat puzzled before their lockers, Ron stood and told them he had something he wanted to say. "This has nothing to do with the game," he said, as he began to choke up.

For the next twenty minutes Ron patiently explained to his teammates that he had diabetes, and explained what the disease was like for him. He told them how he sometimes got dizzy and had to rush into the clubhouse for a candy bar between innings, and that when the team went on the road he had to carry insulin and some syringes so he could give himself a shot.

Then he added, "I don't want this to go outside this room. I expect you to judge me by what I do on the field." He didn't want anyone, his teammates or his fans, to expect less of him just because he had diabetes. That was why he still wanted to keep it a secret from the general public.

Ron's teammates understood. After a few moments one called out, "That's okay, Captain. Let's play ball."

The Cubs did more than just play ball. The team responded with their best season in years. They were in the pennant race until mid-August before running out of steam to finish seventh. Still, their record of 82–80 was an improvement of twenty-three wins from 1962. Ron finished with twenty-five homes runs with ninety-nine RBIs and hit a robust .297. Sadly, however, just before the end of the season the Cubs young second baseman, Ken Hubbs, a close friend of Ron's, was killed when a plane he was piloting crashed. Hubbs's death and a few bad trades kept the team from being a contender over the next few seasons.

Now that his teammates knew about his disease, Ron found that it was easier to live and play with diabetes. Everyone on the team was watching out for him and letting him know when he didn't look well.

Still, the general public had no idea that Ron had diabetes. Although Ron was able to keep his symptoms in check most of the time, there were still occasions when his diabetes caused problems. In one game in the summer of 1968, the Cubs were playing in St. Louis. It was hot and very humid, and toward the end of the game Ron became dehydrated and his blood sugar began to drop.

With the Cubs nursing a one-run lead and a man on second base, Ron warned Cubs pitcher Bill Stoneman to look out for a bunt. Sure enough the next hitter bunted. Stoneman barely moved after the ball. Fortunately, it rolled foul.

Once again Ron warned his pitcher about the bunt. On the next pitch the batter bunted again, and again Stoneman was slow to react. This time however, the ball stayed fair and the runner made third base.

One of the effects of low blood sugar is that it can affect you emotionally, making a person short-tempered. After the play Ron ran over to his pitcher and started yelling at him for not covering the bunt. "Then suddenly it happened," Ron later recalled. "I screamed so loud everything went to my head. They tell me I went to one knee. The guys say I went a little delirious because when Doc came out, I wouldn't let him touch me." At the time, Ron and the Cubs explained away the incident as a combination of Ron's emotional intensity coupled with the effects of the hot weather. In reality, it was probably due to his diabetes.

Later that same year, on September 25, the Cubs were playing the Los Angeles Dodgers in Wrigley Field. Entering the ninth inning the Cubs were losing 1–0 against Los Angeles pitcher Bill Singer. Two men reached base, bringing up Billy Williams. Ron was on deck.

As Ron stood in the batter's circle, he looked up and suddenly saw three scoreboards. He realized that was a warning sign that his blood sugar was low. He felt lightheaded and knelt with one knee on the ground, hoping Billy Williams would get a hit and end the game. But Singer worked Williams carefully and the hitter fouled off several pitches before finally walking, loading the bases. Now Ron would have to bat.

As he described it later, he was feeling so weak that he

"decided to swing at whatever Singer threw." The pitcher wound up and released the ball and as it left his hand Ron saw three baseballs headed toward the plate. "I swung at the middle one," he said later.

"Boom!" He somehow made contact and the ball sailed over the left field fence as the crowd went crazy. The Cubs would win—if Ron could make it around the bases.

Ron was afraid he would pass out on the way and his home run trot turned into a sprint. As he later put it, "I took off like the Olympic 440 relay."

Ahead of him, however, Billy Williams was jogging slowly. He didn't know Ron was in trouble. As Ron raced behind him, he started screaming at Williams, "Go faster, go faster!" Williams did, and by the time Ron made it to the dugout he could barely speak. He sat on the bench and had to eat a candy bar before he could join his teammates in their celebration in the clubhouse.

Despite occasional problems with his disease, Ron became a perennial All-Star, a Gold Glove winner for his defense, and a fan favorite. They loved his fiery play and determination. Ron hardly ever missed a game and played in one hundred sixty or more games seven times, something that few players are able to do. Although he was unable to lead the Cubs to a World Series, they were contenders and Ron helped a new generation of fans discover the joys of Wrigley Field and Cubs baseball.

Still, Ron didn't want anyone to feel sorry for him. Even though he continued to keep his disease a secret to everyone except his family and teammates, he made occasional trips to the hospital to visit with children who were struggling with diabetes, later writing that "Unless you have been young and ill with such a disease, you can't appreciate the apprehension that can exist in the mind of a youngster in this condition. The stories of courage of the young people I've met could fill a book in itself. The children who have juvenile diabetes have a special place in my heart." Ron knew exactly how they felt.

On August 28, 1971, after twelve years as a Cub, Ron was honored with his own day at Wrigley Field.

Traditionally, when a team holds a day for a player, the player receives all sorts of gifts at a pregame ceremony. But when Cubs general manager John Holland told Ron about their plans, Ron asked Holland that any donations in his name be given to a diabetes charity.

Holland readily agreed. "Think of how many diabetics you can help," he said. "When they realize what you've been able to accomplish, it will inspire them to live life as fully as you have."

Ron and the Cubs made the announcement at a press conference. They sold "Ron Santo Day" buttons to benefit diabetes charities, and the night before the game they held a diabetes fund-raising dinner. Ron's teammates, Chicago sportswriters, fans, and Cubs supporters also made donations.

At the pregame ceremony on August 28, Ron still received a number of gifts from the Cubs and his teammates, but as one sportswriter commented, "The big winner was the Diabetes Association of Chicago," which received a check for twenty-five thousand dollars, as well as many smaller donations. Before Ron spoke, a Cubs broadcaster read a letter from President Richard Nixon commending Ron for his work with children with diabetes.

Ron was overwhelmed. He gave a brief speech but after only a few words was too overcome with emotion to continue. "This wasn't a day," he said later. "This was a lifetime."

By letting the world know that he had diabetes, thousands of fans learned about the disease and began to understand just how difficult it had been for Ron to play.

More important, however, they learned that it was possible to live a fulfilling life with the disease. Although a diagnosis of diabetes would change a person's life, it need not ruin it.

As Ron later wrote, "My life changed that day . . . I always thought I'd make my biggest mark as a ballplayer, but it was after I started speaking up about diabetes that I really made a difference." Now that his secret was out he began to make many more hospital visits to children with diabetes, telling them, as he put it, "that they could accomplish anything they wanted despite their disease."

Ron's baseball career continued through the 1974 season. He then retired as one of the best players of his generation and one of the best players in Cubs history, a nine-time All-Star, earning the nickname "Mr. Cub." Beginning in 1990 he then became a popular broadcaster for the Cubs.

He was right when he said that he made the most difference speaking out about diabetes. After retiring as a player Ron worked tirelessly to raise awareness about the disease. Beginning in 1974 he sponsored the annual Ron Santo Walk to Cure Diabetes and helped raise sixty million dollars for diabetes research. A man named Bill Holden, inspired by Ron, walked 2,100 miles from Arizona to Chicago and on the way raised $250,000 for diabetes research.

Due to the efforts of Ron and many others, today a diagnosis of diabetes is not nearly as frightening as it was when Ron first learned that he had the disease. Doctors and researchers have learned much more about diabetes and treatment is easier. Researchers have developed ways for patients to monitor their own blood sugar levels and to give themselves insulin through a shot, an insulin "pen" that delivers a dose by way of a cartridge, or an insulin pump or pod that automatically delivers insulin into the bloodstream. With the help of adults, even young children can now manage their own diabetes.

Ron didn't suffer from more serious diabetes complications until the last few years of his life. He had several heart attacks and underwent heart surgery, and both legs were amputated due to circulation problems caused by diabetes. But that didn't stop Ron. He kept living his life—rooting for the Cubs and working for diabetes awareness—until he passed away at age seventy on December 3, 2010.

Over the last decade of his life Ron's fans started a campaign to get him elected to the National Baseball Hall of Fame. Although many historians feel that Ron belongs in the Hall, he just missed making it.

That hardly matters, because Ron Santo is a solid member of another hall of fame, one that honors people not for what they did on the playing field, but for what they did with their lives off the field. Ron Santo, by his example, showed millions of people that it was possible to live a full life with diabetes. Today, dozens of athletes with diabetes, such as Chicago Bears quarterback Jay Cutler, Tampa Bay Rays outfielder Sam Fuld, Toronto Blue Jays pitcher Brandon Morrow, and golfer Kelli Kuehne, play pro sports.

As his teammate Hall of Famer Ernie Banks once wrote, "Ronnie had all the qualities you look for in someone you would want to carry the name 'Mr. Cub.' As a player, he was a great competitor, a hard worker and a leader. He had intensity. He was determined and ambitious. He wanted to win more than anybody I've ever known.

"Ronnie has handled his own ailment like the true champion he is. He is the most courageous person I've ever been around. I'm inspired by him and by his spirit. He is one of my idols, one of my heroes."

Today children who are diagnosed with diabetes don't have to ask, "Will I still be able to play baseball?" or any other sport. The answer is "Yes!" Ron Santo proved that.

In 1993, pitcher Jim Abbott, who due to a birth defect was born without a right hand, threw a no-hitter for the New York Yankees. Abbott was in the major leagues from 1989 to 1999.

JIM ABBOTT: JUST ANOTHER ONE-ARMED WONDER

WHEN MIKE AND KATHY ABBOTT got their first look at their newborn son, their hearts were filled with joy. Like most new parents, they had big dreams for their first child.

Then they noticed something. Their son's right arm was much shorter than his left arm. In fact, it stopped in a small stump just below the elbow. Apart from one small, misshapen finger, their son had no right hand.

Soon afterwards Mike and Kathy made the most important decision of their son's life: they decided to give the little boy they named Jim their full love and support and treat him the same as they would any other child. While they realized their son might face some difficulties growing up with only one hand, they decided to allow Jim the opportunity to succeed or fail on his own.

No one knows exactly why Jim Abbott was born with only one hand. In the United States, about 120,000 children are born each year with a birth defect, a problem that develops while a baby is growing during pregnancy. Scientists believe that many birth defects are caused by genetic defects, but why they happen is often a mystery. In Jim Abbott's case, why he was born with a missing hand wasn't nearly as important as how he would learn to live with it.

When Jim was growing up in Flint, Michigan, his parents treated him like any other young child. As a toddler Jim hardly even realized he was different from other kids. Growing up with one hand was normal to Jim.

Still, when Jim was five years old, he was fitted with a prosthetic arm, or an artificial arm. The prosthetic arm was equipped with clamping hooks at the end, instead of a hand. Jim's doctor believed that, with practice, Jim could use the clamps as a second hand and that it might help him do things like zip up a jacket or pull on a pair of boots.

Jim, however, had other ideas. Even at age five he was already accustomed to doing things with one hand, and trying to use the clamps made him feel awkward and clumsy. Besides, when he wore the prosthesis he felt as if everyone was staring at him. After Jim spent a year trying to adjust to his artificial arm, Jim's parents allowed him to stop wearing it. That made Jim much happier.

The older he became, the more Jim realized that there wasn't anything he couldn't learn to do with one hand. Jim went to a regular school and took the same classes as everyone else. When he did reach an obstacle, there was always someone who would try to help him learn to overcome it. For example, one of Jim's teachers at his school helped him learn to tie his shoes one-handed. It took Jim longer to learn than other kids, but he figured it out.

Despite having only one hand, Jim was very athletic. His parents thought that because he had only one hand that soccer might be the best sport for him to play, but Jim didn't like soccer very much.

On the other hand, Jim *loved* baseball. The Detroit Tigers were Jim's favorite team. He loved watching the Tigers on television and from the time he was a young boy he dreamed about playing in the major leagues. Although his parents worried that the game might be difficult for him, Jim didn't feel that way, and they never discouraged him. Jim never thought about what he couldn't do. As he later said, "I always believed that there was a way to get things done, no matter what the circumstances."

When Jim was old enough his parents bought him a baseball glove for his left hand and Mike Abbott began playing catch with his son. At first it was awkward. Learning to catch a ball in a glove takes a lot of practice, and it is hard enough to learn to play catch with both hands. It was even more difficult for Jim.

He had to figure out how to catch the ball with the glove on his left hand and then throw it. Over time, Jim figured out that he could balance the glove on the end of his right arm as he wound up and threw the ball. Then, as soon as he let go of the ball, he slipped his left hand into the glove so he could catch the return throw. After catching the ball, he would slide the glove under the crook of his right arm, pull his hand out, grab the ball, and balance the glove on the end of his right arm again.

That might sound complicated, and it is. At first it was awkward for Jim and frustrating. Jim sometimes dropped his glove, or the ball would slip from his fingers. Yet each day he got a little bit better. Soon he didn't even have to think about what he was doing.

When his dad was at work, Jim practiced by himself. Outside the Abbott's townhouse, Jim would throw a ball against a brick wall for hours, pretending he was on the mound playing for the Tigers. Each time he wound up and threw the ball, he would have to slip his left hand into the glove so he could field the ball as it bounced back. With repetition, the movement became so smooth and natural looking that others couldn't figure out how Jim managed to do it so quickly. As Jim said later, playing catch with one hand soon became "very natural to me, and very easy."

Jim learned to play other sports one-handed as well. He learned to swing a bat by choking up a little more than most hitters, learned to dribble and shoot a basketball, and learned to throw a football. He was one of the best athletes in his neighborhood and spent hours every day playing with his friends. Still, every once in a while Jim would be taunted because of his missing hand. Sometimes other kids called him "Crab," or other cruel names.

Jim just tried to ignore them. If anything, the taunts only made Jim want to succeed even more. "My disability pushed me to work harder," he later said. "As a kid I really wanted to fit in, sports became a way for me to gain acceptance." Once the other kids saw that teasing didn't make Jim angry, they usually stopped. Besides, Jim was often the best athlete on the playground. His mother later said that "Jim has always been well adjusted, self-motivated—

academically and in sports. After a while, what he did we took for granted."

Despite Jim's disability, when he started playing Little League baseball he was one of the best players in his league. When Jim turned eleven, his coach noticed that he had one of the best arms on the team and suggested that he try pitching.

All the hours Jim had spent throwing against the brick wall paid off. In his first game as he stood on the mound and warmed up, he didn't even have to think about what he was doing. He transferred his hand into the glove effortlessly after every pitch. He wasn't thinking about pitching with one arm. He just concentrated on throwing the ball over the plate and getting the batter out.

After only a few pitches the players on the other team and the parents watching from the stands forgot that they were watching a one-armed pitcher. The only difference between Jim and the other pitchers in the league was that Jim was better! He threw a no-hitter in his very first game. Although his parents knew Jim was talented, they could hardly believe what he had just done. "We were amazed," his mother later recalled.

Word about the great one-armed pitcher soon spread and everyone encouraged Jim to continue playing. Baseball still wasn't easy for him, but he kept trying and slowly kept improving. Hitting a baseball was difficult, particularly as he grew older and had to face pitchers who threw almost as hard as he did. As a thirteen-year-old Jim played the entire season without getting a single hit. On the mound, however, he was still terrific. By the time he reached ninth grade and was able to play on the freshman team at Central High School, Jim was one of the best pitchers his age in the city of Flint.

Still, some people looked at Jim and thought of what he could not do, rather than what he could. They found it hard to believe that as Jim got older and faced better competition he could continue to compete. Even Jim's coach, Mr. Holec, worried that at some point Jim might have to stop playing.

One day when Jim was pitching, Mr. Holec was talking to Jim's dad about Jim's future in the game. Although Jim had a strong arm, Coach Holec worried that he might not be able to react quickly enough as a fielder. Holec was afraid that as Jim pitched against bigger and stronger hitters, he might not be able to protect himself from balls hit hard directly at him. He was afraid Jim might get hurt.

As the two men talked they heard the sharp sound of the bat striking the ball. The hitter laced a hard line drive into the ground between home plate and the pitcher's mound. The ball ricocheted toward Jim, a hit known as a one-hopper.

One-hoppers are difficult for any pitcher to field. There is no time to think, only to react.

The next thing Coach Holec and Mike Abbott saw was Jim calmly throwing the ball to first base. Jim had learned to transfer the glove to hand so quickly that he had easily fielded the hard hit ground ball and threw the runner out by a mile. Coach Holec just looked at Jim's dad and said, "Well, I guess he can handle grounders back at him."

Still, opposing teams tried to test Jim, particularly when he was pitching well. In one game his freshman year, Jim dominated. Hitter after hitter found Jim's fastball impossible to hit. Halfway through the game Jim already had ten strikeouts.

Then the coach on the other team had an idea. He wondered how well Jim could field a bunt with only one arm. He ordered the next hitter to try a bunt.

Jim wound up and threw, making the smooth move to put his glove on his hand an instant after he let go of the ball. The batter squared around, and holding his bat level, allowed the ball to strike the bat. It bounced feebly on the ground between Jim and the baseline.

Jim reacted quickly, scooping the ball up with his glove, pinning it against his body, then taking the ball out and throwing to first base. This time, however, Jim tried to be too quick, and did not make the transfer smoothly. The batter streaked down the line and beat Jim's throw.

The manager of the other team thought he had found Jim's weak spot. He ordered the next hitter to bunt. In fact, he ordered the next seven hitters to bunt.

Wrong! Jim cleanly fielded each of the next seven bunts and easily threw out the runners. Jim didn't even mind that the coach had tested him with the bunts, later joking that "I don't know if that was the situation with one hand, or because I'd just struck out ten of them." Word soon got around that Jim Abbott didn't have a weak spot. Having just one hand made no difference in his performance.

Jim was discovering that he could do just about anything he wanted, if he practiced enough. Coach Holec encouraged Jim, with his strong arm, to try out for the football team as a quarterback. Although it took Jim a while to figure out how to take the snap from center without dropping it, Jim soon adapted and led his team to the state semifinals.

Still, however, baseball remained his best sport. When Jim wasn't pitching, he played outfield, and he even became a good hitter, once cracking a game-winning home run over the center field fence three hundred thirty feet away. And as more people in and around Flint became aware of the way Jim had learned to adapt to playing with one hand, parents often took their children with similar physical problems and disabilities to see Jim pitch. Jim would go out of his way to meet with such children and give them words of encouragement.

By the time Jim was a senior in high school, he was one of the best pitchers in the state of Michigan. He threw his fastball more than ninety miles per hour and it had a natural break that made it even more difficult to hit. In his final year of high school he threw four no-hitters and struck out an amazing one hundred forty-eight batters in only seventy-four innings, finishing the year with an earned run average of only 0.76.

By then, major league baseball scouts were watching Jim nearly every time he took the mound. They weren't very concerned that he had only one hand. All they knew was that Jim could get hitters out.

Jim wanted to play professionally, but at the same time he also wanted to go to college. The University of Michigan offered Jim a baseball scholarship, and Jim accepted. Still, even though they knew he was going to attend college, the

Toronto Blue Jays still selected Jim in the baseball draft, just in case he changed his mind. Jim was flattered, and the Blue Jays' offer was tempting, but Jim had made a commitment. He also knew that if he performed well at Michigan he might still have an opportunity to play pro baseball.

Jim did just that. From the first time he took the mound at Michigan, Jim was one of the best collegiate pitchers in the country. In three years he posted a 26–8 mark with a 3.03 ERA. He was twice named Michigan's Most Valuable Pitcher, was selected as the left-handed pitcher on the *Sporting News* collegiate all-star baseball team, and won the Sullivan Award as the top amateur athlete in the United States.

When he became eligible again for the major league draft after his junior year, he was picked in the first round by the California Angels, the eighth player selected overall. Jim was excited about being drafted, but before he signed with the Angels he still had some more pitching to do. In the summer of 1988 he made the U.S. Olympic baseball team and was the winning pitcher in the gold medal game against Japan in the Summer Olympics in Seoul, South Korea.

After the Olympics Jim signed with the Angels. It was

too late in the year for him to pitch anymore so the Angels told Jim to get ready for spring training the following year.

When Jim arrived at spring training in February of 1989, he was a big story because of his hand. It seemed as if every newspaper in the country wanted to do a story on Jim and he patiently answered the same questions over and over. Yet as spring training went on, Jim started getting attention not because of his missing right hand, but because of the way he threw the baseball with his left hand.

Despite having no professional experience and being one of the youngest players in spring training, each time Jim took the mound it was clear that he was one of the best pitchers in the Angels camp. Very few players go directly from amateur baseball to the major leagues without playing in the minor leagues first. The Angels had not expected Jim to make the major league team, but the more manager Doug Radar and pitching coach Marcel Lachemann saw Jim throw, the more they believed that he deserved to be in the starting rotation. His fastball touched ninety-four miles per hour, and he also threw a hard slider and a curveball, all with good control. Although most young pitchers are not mature enough to go straight to the major leagues, the Angels knew that Jim's time on the

Olympic team, coupled with his experiences as a one-armed player, had helped him to grow up quickly.

Just before the end of spring training Lachemann approached Jim in the hotel where he was staying and told Jim he had made the Angels starting rotation. Jim later described it as "the happiest day of my life." But there were more happy days to come—as well as a few that were not so pleasant.

Jim wasn't the first player missing a limb to play in the major leagues. In 1945 outfielder Pete Gray, who lost his arm in a train accident, played one season for the St. Louis Browns. That same year pitcher Bert Shepard briefly pitched in the big leagues after losing his leg in World War II. But no pitcher with one arm had ever made it to the majors.

Jim made history in his regular season debut on April 8 at the Angels home park in Anaheim, California. They were playing the Seattle Mariners. Nearly fifty thousand people, one of the biggest crowds of the season, crammed into the ballpark. Everyone wanted to see Jim pitch.

Jim tried to downplay the fact that he was the first one-armed pitcher in baseball. He just wanted to be seen as a pitcher.

Before the game Jim sat with veteran pitcher Bert

Blyleven in the clubhouse. Blyleven was nearing the end of a wonderful career that would one day earn him election to the Baseball Hall of Fame. Like Jim, Blyleven had once been a highly touted rookie. The first batter he ever faced in the big leagues had hit a home run.

Just before Jim left for the field Blyleven turned to him and said, "Savor the moment." Then he paused and added, "And win the game."

When Jim warmed up, the crowd buzzed with excitement. As he threw his first pitch to Seattle leadoff hitter Harold Reynolds, flashbulbs from cameras all over the ballpark went off as fans tried to capture Jim's first pitch.

The slider snaked over the plate as Reynolds kept his bat on his shoulder.

"Strike!" called out the umpire. The crowd roared its approval. Unfortunately, Jim and the Angels gave them little to cheer about after that. Two pitches later Reynolds singled. The next hitter also got a base hit and then Jim threw a wild pitch. Although he settled down after that, both runners scored on ground balls. A few errors by the Angels didn't help and Jim was pulled from the game in the fifth inning as California lost, 7–0.

Jim was disappointed and admitted, "There was definitely some nervousness. I wish I could do it over again," but the Angels still liked what they saw. "I thought that under the conditions he was outstanding," said manager Doug Radar. Seattle's Harold Reynolds told a reporter that even though he got a hit off Abbott "he threw a hard slider and I was impressed."

But not everyone agreed with Radar. After Jim lost his next start, some observers began to say that he wasn't ready for the majors. They accused the Angels of rushing him to the big leagues to take advantage of the publicity he attracted as a one-armed pitcher.

Jim didn't agree, but as he later put it, "I didn't feel like I was earning my keep." He knew that until he proved he could win in the major leagues that some people would still wonder if it was possible for a pitcher with a disability like his to succeed. Besides, Jim didn't just want to be known as the first one-armed pitcher in the major leagues. He wanted to be known as a good pitcher who happened to have only one arm.

Jim took the mound in his next start against the Baltimore Orioles determined to prove those who doubted him wrong.

This time, Jim was in command from the start and the Angels, who had been shut out in Jim's first two starts, helped him out by scoring a few runs. Jim pitched six strong innings while giving up only two runs as the Angels won 3–2. Jim was happy, and relieved.

With his first win under his belt Jim was able to relax and just concentrate on pitching. He finished the season with a record of 12–12 and came in fourth in balloting for the American League's Rookie of the Year award. Then, after winning ten games in his second season, in 1991 Jim won eighteen games and finished third in voting for the Cy Young award as the best pitcher in the league. Fans almost forgot that Jim was pitching with only one arm. They just considered him a good pitcher, period.

But to young people who had lost a limb, Jim was a hero, someone they looked up to as proof that it was possible to be different and still be successful. Jim often met with such young people and told them, "Never allow the circumstances of your life to become an excuse. People will allow you to do it. But I believe we have a personal obligation to make the most of the abilities we have. The focus has to remain on what has been given, not what has been taken away. It is the only choice." That's just what Jim had done.

After the 1992 season, Jim was traded to the New York Yankees. Although he knew he would miss his teammates, he was excited to be joining the Yankees. After a few down years, the team seemed poised to make a playoff run.

Unfortunately, Jim didn't pitch as well as he hoped for New York. After five years in the majors his fastball wasn't quite as fast as it had once been. Instead of overpowering hitters, Jim had to adjust his pitching style and out-think the batters. But it wasn't easy to change while pitching in the major leagues. In August, as the Yankees battled for the division lead, Jim pitched one of the worst games of his major league career, giving up ten hits and seven runs in less than four innings.

Jim was beginning to doubt himself. For the first time as a professional baseball player, having only one arm began to be a problem. Because of the way Jim had to wind up with just one arm, he couldn't hide the way he held the baseball in his glove. When he had to throw certain pitches, it was hard to keep the other team from seeing what he was going to throw. Without a great fastball he had to out-think the batter and put each pitch in exactly the right place. He was beginning to wonder if he could continue to succeed.

Nevertheless, in his next start against Cleveland, Jim was determined to stay positive. He thought back and re-membered the hard times from his past, like the season he went without getting a hit. He had to tell himself the same things he was usually telling other disabled children, to work hard and believe in himself.

The game got off to a rough start. Jim's first pitch got past the catcher and sailed to the backstop, and he walked Cleveland's first hitter, the speedy Kenny Lofton. This was definitely not the way he wanted to start.

He knew he could not afford another walk and worked the second hitter carefully. His control improved, and when he threw a low fastball, the batter beat the ball into the ground and the Yankee infield turned a double play to get Jim out of trouble.

That's the way the first few innings went. Jim kept the Indians off balance and they kept beating the ball into the ground, where the Yankees infielders made play after play. Meanwhile, the Yankee hitters teed off against Cleveland's pitcher and took a 4–0 lead.

When Jim walked onto the field for the seventh inning, the Yankee Stadium crowd stood and cheered. The scoreboard told the story. He was throwing a no-hitter! Jim was excited, but he tried to stay calm. He still needed nine more outs.

With one out in the seventh, Indian's slugger Albert Belle came to the plate. Jim made a rare mistake and left a pitch over the plate. Belle ripped it down the third base line.

Yankee third baseman Wade Boggs simply reacted, diving to his right and sticking out his glove. The ball met the glove as Boggs went sprawling, then he jumped to his feet and gunned the ball to first base.

Out! The throw just beat Belle to the base and the crowd roared. There are usually a few great plays in every no-hitter, and Boggs had just provided one. Jim got out of the inning and then set the Indians down in order in the eighth. He took the mound in the ninth needing only three more outs for a no-hitter, one of the rarest events in baseball and every pitcher's dream.

Kenny Lofton led off for Cleveland. One of the fastest players in the game, Lofton squared around and tried to bunt for a hit, but the ball rolled foul.

The crowd booed. They thought Lofton might be trying to take advantage of Jim, and didn't think it was fair to try to break up a no-hitter with a bunt. But it didn't bother Jim. He knew that Lofton was just trying to do his job and get on base. Besides, as Jim had proven many years before, he fielded bunts as well as any pitcher in baseball. Lofton swung at the next pitch and grounded out to second base.

Now the crowd really started cheering. Light-hitting Felix Fermin came to bat. He ripped the ball to center field.

Yankees outfielder Bernie Williams had been playing

shallow. Now he turned around and ran back as fast as he could. Jim could only watch as the fate of his no-hitter hung in the air over Williams's head. Then he saw Williams reach up with his glove . . .

And the ball settled in! Two outs!

Everyone in Yankee Stadium was standing and cheering as Jim took the sign from catcher Matt Nokes and looked in at Cleveland's Carlos Baerga. The Cleveland second baseman wasn't going to make it easy on Jim. A switch hitter, Baerga usually hit right-handed against a left-handed pitcher like Jim, but this time he decided to take a chance and hit from the left side. If he hit a slow ground ball, he would be a little closer to first base and might be able to beat it out for a hit.

Baerga swung late and bounced the ball past the mound to Jim's right. He reached for the ball but it eluded his grasp. Yankee shortstop Randy Velarde charged the ball as Baerga raced to first. Then Velarde fielded the ball and threw in one motion. Yankees first baseman Don Mattingly stretched out to receive the throw. Jim turned to watch as every fan held his or her breath and Baerga raced across the first base bag.

The umpire hesitated, and then threw his fist in the air. "Out!"

Jim raised his arm in triumph as his teammates surrounded him and lifted him in the air. Jim had just thrown a no-hitter, one of the very few pitchers in major league baseball history to do so. He had proven beyond every shadow of doubt what it was possible to accomplish. He wasn't just a great one-armed pitcher. He was a great pitcher, period.

Jim played in the major leagues for ten years before retiring. Since leaving baseball he has dedicated his life to helping other people learn to overcome challenges and earns a living as a motivational speaker, telling people his story.

Jim doesn't think he did anything special, and even though others look up to him for his accomplishments, he doesn't feel like a hero. He gives his parents all the credit for providing him with the opportunity to learn what he could do.

"If there was ever any courage in anything I ever did," Jim once said in an interview, "it came from my parents. Their determination to allow me to experience all that life has to offer surely caused them some worry. But I can't think of a greater gift. They never shielded me from anything I ever wanted to do."

Outfielder Curtis Pride was born deaf. Nevertheless he reached the major leagues and between 1993 and 2006 played for several teams and never let his deafness stop him. He is now baseball coach at Gallaudet University.

CURTIS PRIDE: PROUD TO BE A BIG LEAGUER

ONE DAY WHEN CURTIS PRIDE was at bat during a minor league game, he was grazed by a pitch as he turned to get out of the way. Curtis dropped his bat and started to jog to first base. After only a few steps, however, the base umpire waved him back toward home plate. There he saw the home plate umpire gesturing and talking.

Curtis walked up to the umpire, then reached out and lifted the umpire's mask from his face. The plate umpire, who had not umpired one of Curtis's games before, jumped back, angry. Players are not allowed to touch umpires.

The umpire pointed at Curtis, then pointed toward the dugout. He threw Curtis out of the game for touching him.

Curtis stood there for a second, puzzled, then slowly

started to walk away. He couldn't understand what he had done to make the umpire so mad. Then he saw his teammates laughing, and his manager, a big smile on his face, running out onto the field. His manager went up to the umpire and started talking to him. Soon the umpire began to smile and waved Curtis back to the plate, as Curtis's manager turned to face him and explain what had taken place. Then Curtis smiled too.

The plate umpire had not known that Curtis Pride was deaf. When the umpire had tried to explain why he wanted Curtis to come back to home plate, Curtis could not hear what the umpire was saying. So he reached out and lifted the umpire's mask so he could see his lips. Curtis wasn't being disrespectful. He simply needed to see the speaker's lips to understand what was being said. Once Curtis's manager explained to the umpire that Curtis was simply trying to read his lips, the umpire understood. Although the umpire did not think Curtis had been hit by the pitch, he was allowed to stay in the game.

A little understanding and a little opportunity is all Curtis Pride ever needed to reach his goal of playing professional baseball. As a deaf person, he had a more difficult path to the major league than hearing players did, but it was not impossible. His talent and desire have spoken loud and clear to everyone.

★ ★ ★

When their young son Curtis was about six months old, John and Sallie Pride noticed something was different. Although he cried and smiled like most babies, and loved being held and tickled, Curtis didn't make any of the babbling sounds most babies do as they begin to learn how to speak. The Pride's other child, Curtis's sister Jackie, had been making all sorts of different sounds by the age of six months.

At first the Prides didn't know what to think. Then they noticed that loud noises didn't bother Curtis. If he was asleep in his crib and a door slammed shut, Curtis never stirred. If his mother or father called his name when he was awake, Curtis never turned his head.

A short time later the Prides took their son to the doctor to learn if anything was wrong. Several months later Curtis was diagnosed with sensorineural deafness, which meant that he was almost completely deaf. The condition was caused by a measles infection his mother contracted during an epidemic in 1968 while she was pregnant with Curtis.

He had become infected as well, and the infection had damaged the cells in his ear. There simply were not enough sensory cells in his ear to properly transmit sound waves to his brain. Even with the help of hearing aids Curtis would be able to hear only 5 percent of the sound waves that entered his ear. Even then, he wouldn't hear anything very clearly.

When Curtis's parents left the hospital they were very upset. They had no idea how to raise a deaf child. "I remember coming out of the children's hospital after the diagnosis and feeling very negative about the prospects for Curt's future," recalled Curtis's father. Still, the Prides were committed to their son. "As parents, it was our responsibility to give him a chance," said his mother.

Curtis was fortunate that both his parents were accustomed to helping and working with others. His father, John, had been a track star in college at Capital University in Columbus, Ohio, and worked as a consultant in human resources, and his mother, Sallie, was a nurse. They were determined to do everything they could for their son.

The Prides immediately enrolled Curtis in a special program at the hospital for children with hearing impairments and they both read everything they could about deafness so they could provide all the help Curtis would need. They learned that with therapy and training Curtis could learn to speak and as he grew up he could learn to read lips. Although it would not be easy, if those around Curtis understood his condition and were willing to make a few adjustments, he could live a full and active life.

The Prides began helping Curtis right away. His parents and sister made sure they faced Curtis when they spoke to him so he could see their lips move. His mother also made flash cards with words and pictures to help Curtis understand and learn. The Prides even moved from Washington, D.C., to Silver Spring, Maryland, so Curtis could take advantage of special programs offered in the school system.

Like his dad, Curtis was also a good little athlete. From the start, however, the Prides realized that competing in sports would also be a challenge for Curtis. Sound plays a role in nearly everything we do.

Curtis loved to run, and when he was five years old he joined a track team. But when it was time for Curtis to run his first race, the Prides realized that Curtis would not hear the starter's signal that marked the beginning of the race. Sallie Pride explained to the starter that her son was deaf, and then told Curtis that he would have to watch the starter and the other runners to know when it was time to start.

Curtis knelt on the track like all the other kids, but instead of looking straight ahead, he turned his head to look at the starter. A split second after the signal and a half step behind the other kids, Curtis took off. Being deaf might have slowed him at the start, but once Curtis got going no one could stop him. Within a few strides he first caught and then passed the other children and won the race.

Although Curtis had to attend a special program in elementary school for deaf children so he could get the extra help he needed, after school he was just like many other young boys. He loved being with his friends and playing sports.

At age six he joined a T-ball league. Just as they had done at the track program, the Prides had explained to the coaches and other players that Curtis was deaf and might need a little extra attention. They all understood. Most people don't realize that some baseball historians believe that in the early days of baseball the rules were actually changed to help a deaf player named William Hoy. Since Hoy could not hear, when he was at bat he had to turn around after every pitch to learn if it was a ball or strike. Umpires began raising their arm after calling a pitch a strike to help Hoy out.

Curtis loved everything about baseball. After his first game he told his parents, "I'm going to be a baseball player." They just smiled, but Curtis was serious. When he set a goal for himself, he intended to meet it.

Playing sports allowed Curtis to spend time and make friends with children who were not deaf, and he was such a good athlete that, as his mother remembered later, "everybody wanted to have Curtis on their team." As Curtis put it, "Being good at sports boosted my self-esteem and helped me to make friends." In addition to track and baseball, Curtis also participated in other sports like soccer and basketball.

Although he was a good athlete, it was still hard for him. Because he couldn't hear a teammate call out his name for a pass or a referee blow the whistle, Curtis had to pay close attention all the time. Also, other kids had a difficult time understanding his voice, particularly when they first met Curtis. Because deaf people cannot hear themselves talk, they sometimes don't pronounce words as clearly as a hearing person. Because of this people sometimes mistakenly think that deaf people are stupid. Sometimes other kids would make fun of the way Curtis talked. Although he was naturally shy, Curtis understood that until someone got to know him, he sometimes made them uncomfortable. Even though it was difficult he would go out of his way to try to talk with his teammates and other kids, trying to put them at ease and make it easier for them to understand him.

All Curtis wanted was to be like everyone else. Even though he knew that was impossible, he was determined to live as normal a life as possible. Curtis was very bright and learned quickly, but it was still difficult for him to communicate with others, particularly strangers who did not realize he was deaf. But John and Sallie Pride knew that Curtis would have to learn. To help him do so, they made Curtis do things like order food at a restaurant and pay for things at the store, "just like the other kids," she said later. Although others sometimes had a difficult time understanding Curtis's speech, particularly when he was young and just learning to talk, with the help of hand gestures Curtis usually got his point across. Each time he did, he felt a little more comfortable.

★ ★ ★

When it was time for Curtis to enter the seventh grade his parents wanted to send him to a special school for deaf children where he would learn sign language. Many deaf children thrive in such schools.

But Curtis didn't want to leave his friends or go to

special classes for deaf children. Curtis wanted to be in a regular class like everybody else. "I told my parents it was my chance to be independent," said Curtis later, "to function in the normal world."

Curtis's counselors and doctors did not think it was a good idea and told his parents that if they put him in regular school they would be making a big mistake. They were worried that Curtis would be teased and that his teachers might not know how to teach a deaf student. Curtis would be challenged both academically and socially. Students in junior high can sometimes be cruel and they warned Curtis's parents that he might get picked on.

By that time John Pride was working for the government as the director of a research program on mental retardation and had learned that even people with significant mental disabilities are still able to live lives of accomplishment. They decided to give Curtis every opportunity to follow his dreams and allowed him to attend a regular school.

Curtis was thrilled and adapted very quickly. Although he still took speech therapy classes, and sometimes had to remind his teachers to look directly at him when they were speaking, most of the time he was treated like any other student. He made lots of friends and was a standout athlete, and a terrific student. Of course he had to do things a little differently. Because he could only understand his teachers by watching them speak, Curtis couldn't take his own notes when a teacher was talking. Other students shared their notes with him so he could read them over after class. That not only helped Curtis, but made his classmates realize how nice it felt to help others.

Curtis knew that because he was deaf he had to work a little harder than others, but he saw that as a challenge he could overcome. One day in seventh grade he sat down and wrote out a set of forty goals he hoped to achieve in his life. One of those goals was to play major league baseball.

It soon became clear that Curtis was not just one of the best students in his school, he was also one of the best athletes. By the time he started high school at John F. Kennedy High School, Curtis was a star outfielder on the school baseball team, ran for the track team, played point guard on the basketball team, and was a prolific scorer on the soccer team. He also found time to participate in swimming and gymnastics. In fact, Curtis was so good that the only problem he had was deciding what sport to pursue.

·ck Magazine named Curtis as one of the top fifteen _·ccer_ players in the world, and he was selected to be a member of the U.S. National All-Star Soccer Team. He traveled to China to compete for the 1985 Junior World Cup. The College of William and Mary offered Curtis a scholarship to play basketball, and he was also one of the best young baseball players in the country. By Curtis's senior year scouts flocked to his games to watch him play.

An outfielder, Curtis was strong and fast. Baseball scouts looked at him and saw what is known as a five-tool player: someone who can run fast, hit, hit with power, throw, and field. They loved his attitude and were not concerned about his inability to hear. Curtis had learned to adapt.

Because of his deafness, Curtis could not hear the sound of the ball striking the bat or his teammates calling for a ball hit to the outfield. Whereas a hearing player could afford to daydream, Curtis could not. But that actually helped him. As he later said, "I am probably a better baseball player because of my disability than I would be without it. There are a lot of little things that I'm able to recognize that most other baseball players wouldn't."

Although Curtis valued education and accepted a scholarship to play basketball at William and Mary, he also wanted to play baseball. In the summer after his senior year of high school the New York Mets drafted Curtis in the tenth round of the free agent draft of amateur players.

Now Curtis had to decide whether to play basketball or baseball.

Or did he? The more he and his parents thought about it, the more they wondered why he couldn't try to do both. After all, the college basketball season went from late fall though the winter, and baseball was played in the spring and the summer.

The Mets badly wanted Curtis to play baseball, so they agreed to sign him to a contract but still allow him to go to college and play basketball. Once school was over each year Curtis would then join one of the Mets minor league teams. The Mets thought Curtis could be a star. They didn't mind waiting for him.

Soon after he signed with the Mets, and just a few weeks after high school graduation, Curtis's parents drove him to Kingsport, Tennessee, where Curtis was assigned to play for the Mets minor league team. Only seventeen years old, Curtis had never lived on his own.

When his parents left him at the motel where he would live in Kingsport, Curtis looked sad and the Prides almost turned around and took him back home. But they knew Curtis wanted to play baseball.

Once again, Curtis had to help his coaches and teammates learn what it was like to have a deaf ballplayer on the team. At first he felt lonely and left out. When other players hung around the locker room and told jokes and fooled around, Curtis didn't know what they were laughing about.

Fortunately, one of Curtis's teammates understood. He realized that Curtis was feeling left out and he went out of his way to speak with him. "He taught me how to handle myself on the field," said Curtis later. "He introduced me to all the players. Basically, he went around telling the guys that I'm easy to talk to and how they should do it. Pretty soon, they learned to face me . . . Word gets around the world of baseball pretty fast, so everyone soon knew about my disability . . . after they talked to me once, they felt comfortable. Everyone felt at ease."

Still, there were a few teammates who made fun of Curtis and times when he had trouble living on his own. Once when his car broke down a mechanic thought Curtis was mentally challenged and tried to overcharge him.

Curtis tried to look past these incidents and focus on the positives. For the next few years he was incredibly busy, attending college and starting as point guard for the William and Mary basketball team, then playing baseball all summer. He made slow but steady progress in the Mets minor league system, and by the time he graduated with a degree in finance, Curtis was a top prospect.

He was also a role model. Each time he played in a new city, more people would learn about the deaf ballplayer. Deaf and other disabled children would come to the ballpark to meet him and send him letters. Curtis understood how much he could help others and always tried to make time for them. In the off-season he even worked as a special education teacher.

Although Curtis was progressing well, by the end of the 1992 season he had spent seven years in the minor leagues and still had not advanced past double-A baseball, two steps below the major leagues. The Mets had a lot of good players and Curtis was getting impatient.

After that season, since Curtis was not on the Mets major league roster, Curtis was allowed to become a free agent. Now any team in baseball could sign him.

The Nation League Montreal Expos jumped at the chance. Their scouts had been watching Curtis. In his last season in the Mets farm system Curtis had finally started to show some power at the plate and the Expos thought he could be a very good player.

At first they assigned Curtis to their double-A team in

Harrisburg, Pennsylvania. Curtis was determined to prove that he belonged in the major leagues. After all, when he had set those forty goals when he was in seventh grade, he had written down that he wanted to play in the major leagues, not the minors.

Curtis got off to a quick start in Harrisburg and soon became a fan favorite. They became accustomed to seeing Curtis slash a line drive to the outfield for a hit, then take a big lead off first and steal second, or crack a home run with men on base. Fifty games into the season Curtis was hitting a spectacular .356, with twenty-one stolen bases and fifteen home runs. He was too good for double-A baseball. On June 21, the Expos promoted him to their triple-A team in Ottawa, Ontario, in Canada. If he succeeded there, his next stop would be Montreal.

Although the pitchers were better in triple-A, it didn't matter to Curtis. He just kept hitting and stealing bases. He played the rest of the season for the Ottawa Lynx and hit .302, with six more home runs and twenty-nine stolen bases. For the year he hit .324 with fifty-one stolen bases and twenty-one home runs, one of the best performances in the minor leagues.

But Curtis's season wasn't over. Late that summer Montreal general manager Dan Duquette told a reporter that he believed Curtis had "a chance to play every day in the major leagues." When Ottawa's season ended, the Expos called Curtis up to the major leagues.

He was thrilled and just wanted to help his team. The Expos were fighting for the playoffs and Curtis knew he probably would not get a chance to play much. The Expos' three starting outfielders—Marquis Grissom, Larry Walker, and Moisés Alou—were all terrific players. Still, he wanted to help his team in any way he could. Then Expos explained to him that he had to be ready. He might be called on to pinch-run, pinch-hit, or come into the game as a defensive replacement at any time.

Curtis made sure the other Expos outfielders knew the only thing they needed to know when they played with him. Since he couldn't hear other outfielders call for the baseball, when Curtis called to make a catch, they had to let him catch it. Apart from that, they could treat him like any other ballplayer.

On September 14, 1993, soon after he joined the team, the Expos played the Cardinals in St. Louis. Both teams were fighting for a spot in the playoffs. With the Expos leading 10–2 in the eighth inning, Montreal manager Felipe Alou told Curtis to take over in left field.

The St. Louis announcer called out his name and Curtis

took the field. The few Montreal fans in the crowd cheered. Curtis, of course, couldn't hear them. But as he later once said, "One big advantage to being deaf is that I don't hear opposing fans boo me."

The Cardinals immediately rallied to score five runs, but Curtis was flawless in the field, making a long run to catch a foul fly ball and fielding a single.

Then Curtis came up to bat in the eighth inning, facing Cardinals pitcher Todd Burns. He was nervous and swung at the first pitch. He hit a routine fly ball to center field.

The Expos hung on to win. Curtis could now say he was a major league player, but he knew he wouldn't feel like he really belonged until he finally got a base hit and really helped his team win a game.

A few days later, when the Expos returned to Montreal to play the Phillies, Curtis got his chance.

In the eighth inning the Expos trailed the Phillies 7–4. With two runners on and one out, Montreal's pitcher was due to bat. Manager Felipe Alou told Curtis to pinch-hit.

He swung the bat a few times to get loosened then stepped in against relief pitcher Bobby Thigpen. He was a tough pitcher. Only a few years before he had set a major league record by saving fifty-seven games.

More than forty-five thousand fans filled Montreal's

Olympic Stadium. When Curtis stepped to the plate they cheered long and loud. Many of them had heard about the deaf rookie outfielder and even though they knew he couldn't hear them, they wanted him to know that they appreciated how hard he had worked to make the major leagues.

Curtis, of course, was not distracted by the sound. He was focused only on the ball coming out of Thigpen's hand. The pitcher wound up and threw, trying to throw a strike to get ahead of the rookie hitter.

Curtis saw the ball clearly and took a hard swing. Most players know they have hit the ball well by the sound of the bat striking the ball. Curtis couldn't hear that, but he could feel that he had hit the ball square.

The ball rocketed to deep left center field with Phillies center fielder Lenny Dykstra, one of the fastest players in baseball, racing after it. Curtis tore from the batter's box and bolted toward first base.

After only a few steps Dykstra pulled up short. The ball was over his head! It bounded up against the fence in left center field. The two Expos runners raced around the bases and scored as Curtis, arms and legs pumping furiously, ran as hard as he could, pivoting off first base then heading to second, pulling up with a double as the Expos now trailed only 7–6.

The crowd stood and cheered as a tear dripped down Curtis's cheek. Now he felt like a big leaguer. His dream had come true.

Still, he remained focused on the game and stared intently at third base coach Jerry Manuel, waiting for Manuel to give the sign to Curtis and the next hitter. Curtis didn't want to miss a sign in case Manuel wanted him to steal.

But as Curtis stared, Manuel didn't give him a sign, and the crowd didn't stop cheering. Curtis just kept staring at the base coach. Finally Manuel looked at Curtis and, making sure he could see him, mouthed the words, "Tip your hat for the fans." They were not going to stop until Curtis acknowledged them.

Curtis understood. He took his hat off his head, stood on second base, and waved his hat to the crowd, as proud as he had ever been in his life. The crowd cheered itself hoarse.

A few moments later, Curtis raced home on a base hit to tie the game, and the Expos went on to defeat the Phillies. In every way, it had been a special day for Curtis.

After the game, Jerry Manuel summed up everyone's feelings when he said, "There were a lot of teary eyes in our dugout and in the Phillies dugout as well. This was an amazing experience with a special man."

Curtis felt pretty special as well. Even though he was deaf, it hadn't made any difference. He had still made the major leagues. And about those cheers? Although he could not hear them, "I could feel them," he said later, the vibrations from thousands of roars and clapping hands. And that felt very, very good.

Curtis Pride went on to play eleven seasons in the major leagues for the Expos, Detroit Tigers, Boston Red Sox, Atlanta Braves, New York Yankees, and Los Angeles Angels. Today he is a baseball coach at Gallaudet University in Washington, D.C., a college serving deaf and hard-of-hearing students. Curtis also sponsors the Together With Pride Foundation, which helps support and create programs for hearing impaired children that focus on the importance of education and the learning of life skills, along with promoting positive self-esteem.

SOURCES AND FURTHER READING

When I write a book I make use of many different sources of information, including newspaper stories, magazine articles, books, interviews, video documentaries, and the Internet.

If you would like to learn more about any of the athletes or topics discussed in this book, ask your teacher or school or town librarian for help. They can show you how to find newspaper and magazine articles and other information online, and find some of the books and articles listed below, many of which were helpful to me when writing this book. The books may be purchased online or through any bookstore. If your library does not have a copy, the librarian can probably borrow it for you from another library.

Teachers and librarians love helping kids learn, so don't be afraid to ask for help. Happy reading!

MORDECAI "THREE FINGER" BROWN

Books:

Brown, Peter, and Cindy Thompson. *Three Finger: The Mordecai Brown Story*. Lincoln, Nebraska: University of Nebraska Press, 2006.

See also www.mordecaibrown.com.

I also used many old newspaper and magazine stories written about Mordecai.

RON SANTO

Books:

Bronson, Jim. *Ron Santo: 3B.* New York: G.P. Putnam's Sons, 1974.

Santo, Ron, and Randy Minkoff. *Ron Santo: For Love of Ivy.* Chicago: Bonus Books, Inc., 1993.

Articles:

"Ron Santo Battled Daunting Opponent: Diabetes," *Chicago Tribune,* Dec. 4, 2010.

"Ron Santo a Player Unlike Any Other," *Chicago Sun-Times,* Dec. 3, 2010.

"Ron Santo's Secret on the Field," www.guideposts.org/inspirational-stories/inspiring-story-ron-santo-learns -play-baseball-diabetes.

Ron's son Jeff made a terrific film about his father called *This Old Cub.* You can also find film of Ron on YouTube. com.

JIM ABBOTT

Books:

Bernotas, Ben. *Nothing to Prove: The Jim Abbott Story*. New York: Kodansha American, 1995.

Gutman, Bill. *Jim Abbott Star Pitcher*. New York: Grey Castle Press, 1992.

Articles:

"Jim Abbott: Former Left-hand Pitcher Recalls His 1993 No-hitter Against the Cleveland Indians at Yankee Stadium" *Baseball Digest*, May 25, 1987.

"Ace of the Angels," *Sports Illustrated*, Sept. 9, 1991.

"Angel on the Ascent," *Sports Illustrated*, Mar. 13, 1989.

"That Great Abbott Switch," *Sports Illustrated*, May 25, 1987.

"A Special Delivery," *Sports Illustrated*, September 13, 1993.

You can also find video of Jim on YouTube.com.

See also www.jimabbott.net.

CURTIS PRIDE

Although no one has written a book about Curtis, you can find out more about him from these sources:

SOURCES AND FURTHER READING

"Baseball's Pride and Joy," *Sporting News*, May 2, 1994.

"Curtis Pride," *Sports Illustrated*, July 12, 1993.

"Pride of Gallaudet," *Washingtonian*, Oct. 1, 2009.

See also www.togetherwithpride.org.

APPENDIX

MORDECAI BROWN CAREER STATISTICS

FULL NAME: Mordecai Peter Centennial Brown

BORN: October 19, 1876, in Nyesville, Indiana. **DIED:** February 14, 1948

HEIGHT: 5'10" **WEIGHT:** 175 lbs. **BATS:** Both **THROWS:** Right

PITCHING

YEAR	TEAM	W	L	ERA	G	IP
1903	STL	9	13	2.60	26	201.0
1904	CH Cubs	15	10	1.86	26	212.1
1905	CH Cubs	18	12	2.17	30	249.0
1906	CH Cubs	26	6	1.04	36	277.1
1907	CH Cubs	20	6	1.39	34	233.0
1908	CH Cubs	29	9	1.47	44	312.1
1909	CH Cubs	27	9	1.31	50	342.2
1910	CH Cubs	25	14	1.86	46	295.1
1911	CH Cubs	21	11	2.80	53	270.0
1912	CH Cubs	5	6	2.64	15	88.2
1913	CIN	11	12	2.91	39	173.1
1914[+]		14	11	3.52	35	232.2
1915	CH White Sox	17	8	2.09	35	236.1
1916	CH Cubs	2	3	3.91	12	48.1
CAREER		239	130	2.06	481	3172.1

RON SANTO CAREER STATISTICS

FULL NAME: Ronald Edward Santo

BORN: February 25, 1940, in Seattle, Washington. **DIED:** December 3, 2010

HEIGHT: 6'0" **WEIGHT:** 190 lbs. **BATS:** Right **THROWS:** Right

BATTING

YEAR	TEAM	G	AB	R	H	HR	RBI	AVG
1960	CH Cubs	95	347	44	87	9	44	.251
1961	CH Cubs	154	578	84	164	23	83	.284
1962	CH Cubs	162	604	44	137	17	83	.227
1963	CH Cubs	162	630	79	187	25	99	.297
1964	CH Cubs	161	592	94	185	30	114	.313
1965	CH Cubs	164	608	88	173	33	101	.285
1966	CH Cubs	155	561	93	175	30	94	.312
1967	CH Cubs	161	586	107	176	31	98	.300
1968	CH Cubs	162	577	86	142	26	98	.246
1969	CH Cubs	160	575	97	166	29	123	.289
1970	CH Cubs	154	555	83	148	26	114	.267
1971	CH Cubs	154	555	77	148	21	88	.267
1972	CH Cubs	133	464	68	140	17	74	.302
1973	CH Cubs	149	536	65	143	20	77	.267
1974	CH White Sox	117	375	29	83	5	41	.221
CAREER		2243	8143	1138	2254	342	1331	.277

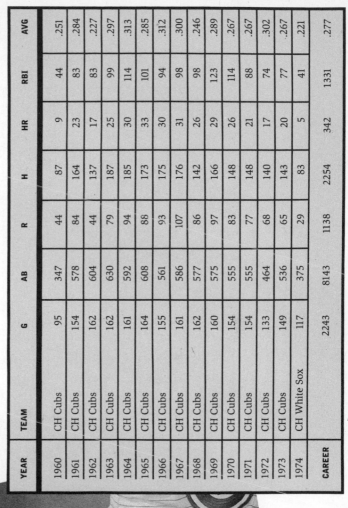

JIM ABBOTT CAREER STATISTICS

FULL NAME: James Anthony Abbott

BORN: September 19, 1967, in Flint, Michigan.

HEIGHT: 6'3"   **WEIGHT:** 210 lbs.   **BATS:** Left   **THROWS:** Left

PITCHING

YEAR	TEAM	W	L	ERA	IP
1989	CAL	12	12	3.92	181.1
1990	CAL	10	14	4.51	211.2
1991	CAL	18	11	2.89	243.0
1992	CAL	7	15	2.77	211.0
1993	NY Yankees	11	14	4.37	214.0
1994	NY Yankees	9	8	4.55	160.1
1995	NYY and CAL	11	8	3.70	197.0
1996	CAL	2	18	7.48	142.0
1998	CH White Sox	5	0	4.55	31.2
1999	MIL	2	8	6.91	82.0
CAREER		87	108	4.25	1674.0

CURTIS PRIDE CAREER STATISTICS

FULL NAME: Curtis John Pride

BORN: December 17, 1968

HEIGHT: 6'0" **WEIGHT:** 210 **BATS:** Left **THROWS:** Right

BATTING

YEAR	TEAM	G	AB	R	H	HR	RBI	AVG
1993	MON	10	9	3	4	1	5	.444
1995	MON	48	63	10	11	0	2	.175
1996	DET	95	267	52	80	10	31	.300
1997[+]	DET/BOS	81	164	22	35	3	20	.213
1998	ATL	70	107	19	27	3	9	.252
2000	BOS	9	20	4	5	0	0	.250
2001	MON	36	76	8	19	1	9	.250
2003	NY Yankees	4	12	1	1	1	1	.083
2004	ANA	35	40	5	10	0	3	.250
2005	LA Angels	11	11	2	1	0	0	.091
2006	LA Angels	22	27	6	6	1	2	.222
CAREER		421	796	132	199	20	82	.250

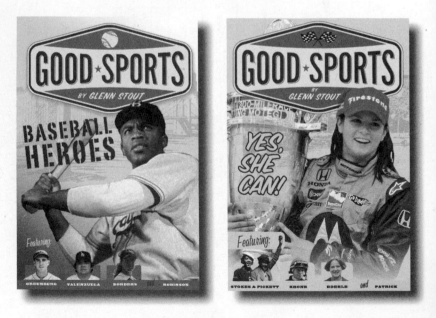

PLAYING FOR THE LOVE OF THE GAME!

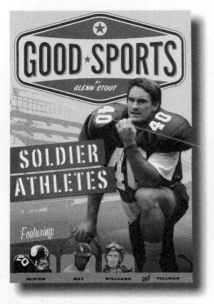

FACT OR FICTION? READ THESE AWESOME NOVELS ABOUT SPORTS AND ATHLETES.

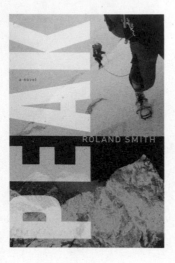

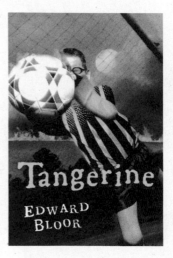

PEAK

The emotional, tension-filled story of a fourteen-year-old boy's attempt to be the youngest person to reach the top of Mount Everest.

TANGERINE

In Tangerine County, Florida, weird is normal. Lightning strikes at the same time every day, a sinkhole swallows a local school, and Paul the geek finds himself adopted into the toughest group around: the middle school soccer team.

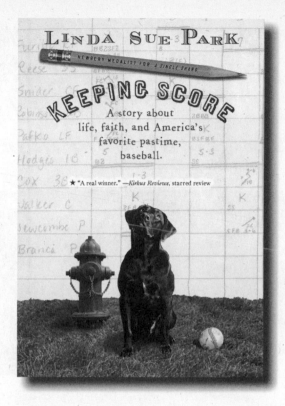

KEEPING SCORE

Nine-year-old Maggie learns a lot about baseball and life in this historical novel set during the Korean War and the Dodgers' 1951 season.

FIND MORE FUN AND FUNNY
BIOGRAPHIES IN THE LIVES
OF . . . SERIES BY KATHLEEN KRULL,
ILLUSTRATED BY KATHRYN HEWITT:

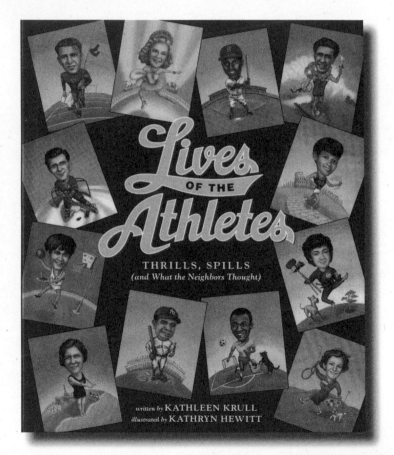

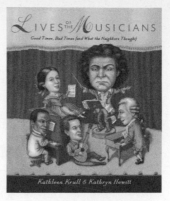

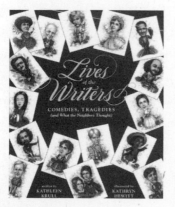

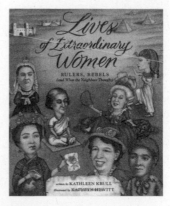

ABOUT THE AUTHOR

When Glenn Stout was growing up outside a small town in central Ohio, he never dreamed that he would become a writer. Then reading changed his life. As a kid, Glenn played baseball, basketball, and football, but baseball was always his favorite sport. Glenn studied poetry and creative writing in college and has had many different jobs, including selling minor league baseball tickets, cleaning offices, grading papers for a college, and painting houses. He also worked as a construction worker and a librarian. Glenn started writing professionally while he was working at the Boston Public Library and has been a full-time writer since 1993. Under the auspices of Matt Christopher, Glenn wrote forty titles in the Matt Christopher sports biography series, and every year he edits *The Best American Sports Writing* collection. Some of Glenn's other books include *Red Sox Century, Yankees Century, Nine Months at Ground Zero*, and *Young Woman and the Sea: How Trudy Ederle Conquered the English Channel and Inspired the World*. He has written or edited more than seventy books.

Glenn is a citizen of both the United States and Canada and lives on Lake Champlain in Vermont with his wife, daughter, two cats, one dog, and a rabbit. He writes in a messy office in his basement, and when he isn't working, he likes to ski, skate, hike in the woods, kayak on the lake, take photographs, and read.